D1442578

SCOOBY-DOO! ™

and the Truth Behind

VAMPIRES

BY MARK WEAKLAND
ILLUSTRATED BY CHRISTIAN CORNIA

CAPSTONE PRESS
a capstone imprint

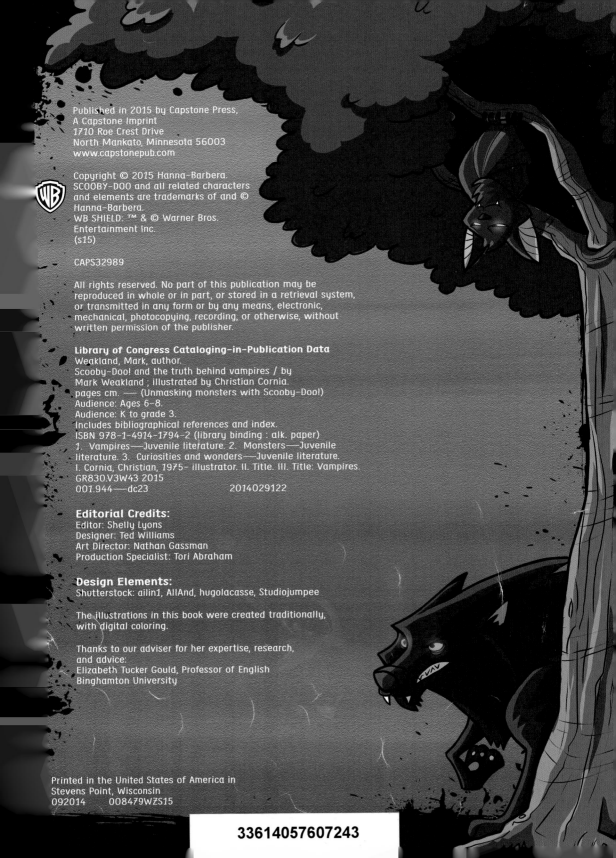

Published in 2015 by Capstone Press,
A Capstone Imprint
1710 Roe Crest Drive
North Mankato, Minnesota 56003
www.capstonepub.com

CAPS32989

Library of Congress Cataloging-in-Publication Data
Weakland, Mark, author.
Scooby-Doo! and the truth behind vampires / by
Mark Weakland ; illustrated by Christian Cornia.
pages cm. —— (Unmasking monsters with Scooby-Doo!)
Audience: Ages 6–8.
Audience: K to grade 3.
Includes bibliographical references and index.
ISBN 978-1-4914-1794-2 (library binding : alk. paper)
1. Vampires——Juvenile literature. 2. Monsters——Juvenile
literature. 3. Curiosities and wonders——Juvenile literature.
I. Cornia, Christian, 1975- illustrator. II. Title. III. Title: Vampires.
GR830.V3W43 2015
001.944——dc23   2014029122

Editorial Credits:
Editor: Shelly Lyons
Designer: Ted Williams
Art Director: Nathan Gassman
Production Specialist: Tori Abraham

Design Elements:
Shutterstock: ailin1, AllAnd, hugolacasse, Studiojumpee

The illustrations in this book were created traditionally,
with digital coloring.

Thanks to our adviser for her expertise, research,
and advice:
Elizabeth Tucker Gould, Professor of English
Binghamton University

Printed in the United States of America in
Stevens Point, Wisconsin
092014   008479WZS15

33614057607243

Daphne, Fred, and Velma were working late. It was time for a snack.

"Let's order a pizza," said Daphne.

"Speaking of pizza, I wonder where Scooby and Shaggy are?" said Fred.

Just then the phone rang. Shaggy was on the line. "Scoob thinks he saw a—"

"Rampire!" barked Scooby.

"That's right, a vampire at the corner of 4th and Main Street," said Shaggy.

"We're on our way!" said Velma.

"Like, how do people become vampires?" asked Shaggy.

"In legends some people are born a vampire," said Daphne.

"But the most common way of becoming a vampire is to get bitten by one," said Fred.

"Ret's get out of here!" said Scooby.

So, if a vampire chases me, how do I escape?" asked Shaggy.

"Carry a bag of rice with you," said Fred. "If you're chased, spill the rice on the ground. A vampire will stop and count each grain!"

"Really?" asked Scooby.

"Bird seed works too," said Velma.

"Like, where do vampires stay?" asked Shaggy.

"In houses and apartments," said Daphne.

"If they're rich they live in mansions and castles!" added Velma.

"During the day they sleep in coffins," said Fred.

Shaggy looked around nervously. "Do vampires have special powers?"

"Special powers?" asked Velma. "Yes. They have unnatural strength."

"And they can hypnotize you with their eyes!" said Fred.

"They can shape-shift too," said Daphne. "They turn into bats, rats, mist, and wolves!"

"Rikes!" said Scooby.

"What are vampires afraid of?" asked Shaggy.

"Many things," said Velma. "Sunlight and running water."

"Fire too!" exclaimed Daphne.

"And crosses," added Fred, "especially silver ones."

"Legends say they're most afraid of a wooden stake through the heart," said Velma. "A stake means the end for a vampire."

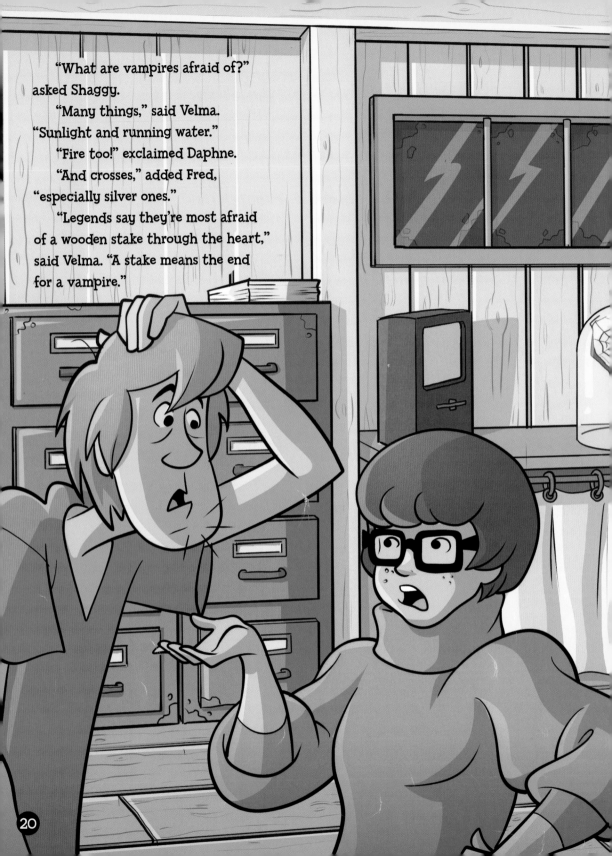

GLOSSARY

canine teeth—long, pointed teeth that help people tear food

coffin—a long container into which a dead person is placed for burial

hypnotize—to put a person into a sleeplike state

legend—a story handed down from earlier times; it is often based in fact, but it is not entirely true

shape-shift—to change physical form at will

READ MORE

Frisch, Aaron. *Vampires*. That's Spooky! Mankato, Minn.: Creative Education, 2013.

Guillain, Charlotte. *Vampires.* Mythical Creatures. Chicago: Raintree, 2011.

Troupe, Thomas Kingsley. *The Legend of the Vampire*. Legend Has It. Mankato, Minn.: Picture Window Books, 2011.

INTERNET SITES

FactHound offers a safe, fun way to find Internet sites related to this book. All of the sites on FactHound have been researched by our staff.

Here's all you do:

Visit *www.facthound.com*

Type in this code: 9781491417942

 Check out projects, games and lots more at
www.capstonekids.com

INDEX